Pa
Adventures

Pacific
Adventures

Jim Cromarty

CF4·K
*Because you're never
too young to know Jesus*

© Copyright 2009 Jim Cromarty
ISBN 978-1-84550-475-5
Published in 2009
by
Christian Focus Publications,
Geanies House, Fearn, Tain
Ross-shire, IV20 1TW,
Great Britain
Cover design by Daniel van Straaten
Cover illustration by Graham Kennedy
Other illustrations by Fred Apps
Printed by MPG Books Ltd, Bodmin, Cornwall

Contents

The Pacific Ocean

God created everything that exists through the Lord Jesus Christ.

The apostle John said of Jesus, 'Through him all things were made; without him nothing was made that has been made' (John 1:3 NIV).

He is the second Person of the Godhead who is 'Father, Son and Holy Spirit' - three Persons, but one God. My God created this world of ours and that included the huge Pacific Ocean.

The Portuguese explorer, Ferdinand Magellan, believed that by sailing west he would discover a short way to the islands of the Far East where he could buy the precious spices that were very popular in Europe. When he found his fleet was blocked by America he sailed south and, in November 1520, rounded the southern tip of South America and into the new ocean which he named, 'Mare Pacificum' - the 'Peaceful Sea.' Magellan died on this expedition, but on 6 September 1522, *Trinidad*, the one remaining sailing boat, with just eighteen sailors, reached Spain. The journey took 3 years and it was the first ship to circle the globe.

The Pacific Ocean is the largest of our oceans measuring approximately 171 million square kilometres, which is about seventeen times the area of the United States of America, and about one third of the surface area of the world. The coastline around the ocean measures approximately 140,000 kilometres.

The average depth of the ocean is over 4,000 metres, while the deepest spot is the Mariana Trench, which is over 11,000 metres below sea level - that's a long way down!

There are three island groups - *Melanesia* which includes Papua New Guinea, Vanuatu, Fiji, and the Solomon Islands; *New Caledonia* which includes Polynesia, New Zealand, Tonga, Samoa, the Easter Islands, and the Pitcairn Islands. Then there is *Micronesia* which includes Nauru, the Marshall Islands, Guam and Palau.

Along the western edge of the Pacific Ocean there is 'the Ring of Fire' which is a strip where there are still active volcanoes. Many

countries in the area suffer earthquakes. Some occur deep down on the ocean floor and cause 'Tsunamis' - waves that race across the ocean at speeds of up to 600 kilometres per hour. When they reach land they flood the coast, washing away homes, crops and people. Some Tsunamis have resulted in the deaths of hundreds of thousands of people who live along the coastal areas.

In the ocean we find about 25,000 islands, most of which are the tops of volcanoes surrounded by coral reefs built by tiny polyps.

Not only does the equator cross the Pacific Ocean, but it is also the only ocean in which we find the International Date Line. This is a most important line, which, with the Greenwich meridian, sets the world's time and days.

Many currents flow across the ocean, one important one being the El Nino. The ocean water heats slightly off the coast of Peru and flows across the Pacific to Australia. This current of warm water affects the climate of many Pacific countries. When it fails to reach Australia the country suffers disastrous droughts.

We should thank God for the rain that falls. He created this world and causes the warm ocean currents to travel many thousands of miles from Peru to Australia's coast.

Try to imagine the amount of water in the Pacific and think of the words of Isaiah 40:12, 'Who has measured the waters in the hollow of his hand, or with the breadth of his hand marked off the heavens? Who has held the dust of the earth in a basket, or weighed the mountains on the scales and the hills in a balance?'

When I go to the beach I can only scoop up about half a cup of the salt water into my hands.

God our Creator

Not everyone believes that God created this amazing world on which we live. My Bible tells me that God created everything through Christ. King Solomon said Jesus was there when the world was created. We read: 'I was there when he set the heavens in place, when he marked out the horizon on the face of the deep, when he established the clouds above and fixed securely the fountains of the deep, when he gave the sea its boundary so that the waters would not overstep his command, and when he marked out the foundations of the earth' (Proverbs 8:27-29).

This creation didn't take billions of years to evolve because my Bible tells me that God created the world in six days (Genesis Chapter 1). As we look about us we begin to understand something about God. Think of the almighty power needed to create the universe. All God had to do was speak and the world was created. The universe tells us something of God's glory, wisdom, love and intelligence. The most glorious of God's creation was man.

Before we look at some of the wonders of the Pacific Ocean region I'd like to tell you about a man named Charles Darwin.

After visiting the Galapagos Archipelago on *HMS Beagle* in 1835, Darwin began to teach that everything in the world 'evolved.' He should have been praising God for the wonderful creation. Instead he claimed that over millions of years one-celled creatures eventually changed and became the living flora and fauna we find in the world today. He said that millions of years ago fish crawled out of the sea and after millions of years some became birds and other land animals. He even suggested that we evolved from monkeys and apes.

Many people believe this to be true, but I'd rather believe what God has told me in the Bible.

The Galapagos Islands are volcanic, some still being active. They are about 1400 kilometres away from Ecuador and near the equator. Darwin found them to be amazing islands with many different plants and animals, but no humans. There are eighty different spiders; 300 different beetles; eighty distinct land snails; 650 different sea shells; 120 types of crabs and a great number of birds and animals.

One amazing animal is the giant tortoise that has been known to live for 150 years. They are so big that they can walk with a

man sitting on their shell. In the ocean surrounding the Galapagos Islands there are many whales, seals, sea lions, penguins, dolphins and a great variety of fish.

You also might see the frigate bird, sometimes called 'The Man O' War.' It's a sea bird yet it doesn't have oil on its feathers. If it landed on the ocean and its feathers became soaked, it couldn't fly. Yet it has a long beak and swoops down to the water in order to grab any fish swimming close to the surface of the ocean.

The frigate steals food from other birds and even steals their nests. When we think about the wonderful variety of animals and plants on the Galapagos Islands and throughout the whole world we should remember the words of Psalm 19:1 - 'The heavens declare the glory of God; and the firmament shows His handiwork.' Everything about creation points to the glory of our God! But God has promised a new heavens and a new earth when Jesus returns. That universe will be flawless and without sin. I pray you will 'Believe on the Lord Jesus Christ, and ... be saved' (Acts 16:31).

The New Hebrides

Of the many island groups found in the Pacific Ocean the New Hebrides is one of the most interesting. This archipelago consists of eighty-two islands, most of which are inhabited and are found in that part of the Pacific Ocean region called 'The Coral Sea.' The islands are largely the tops of extinct volcanoes, although several are still active. The area is hot and wet and surrounding many of the islands we find beautifully coloured coral reefs.

A tree that is well known in that region is the Giant Banyan tree, which grows to almost thirty-five metres in height. On the islands cotton, bananas, coconuts and cocoa are cultivated. Yams are still used for food by the native people. Of all the animals found on the islands, pigs were very important as they were once used by the natives, not just for food, but also as money. Men bought their wives using pigs as the payment.

Deep under the ocean there is what is called 'the New Hebrides Trench' which is where two great sections of the earth meet. When they grate together, earthquakes occur. It is worth remembering that the ocean depth here is 7,570 metres. It would be difficult to catch any fish on the bottom of the ocean in that region. My fishing line isn't long enough.

The capital city is Vanuatu, which means 'Eternal life,' and one of the islands has the Christian name of 'Pentecost.' I wonder why these names were used?

Perhaps its because of the people who came to this area to share the good news of Jesus Christ with the cannibals.

It's hard to believe that people killed and ate other humans. In many parts of the Pacific there were cruel, violent tribes of cannibals who lived on beautiful islands surrounded by coral reefs and blue ocean waters. Despite their lovely surroundings they were frequently involved in warfare with neighbouring tribes. It was a common practice for the victorious warriors to cook and eat their victims believing that the courage and strength of their victims would be passed to them.

During the 19th century Great Britain had experienced great revivals when God poured out His Spirit upon the church and this resulted in a tremendous burst of missionary work by godly men and women. Hudson Taylor started the China Inland Mission. Many missionaries went to India and other Asian countries.

One of the best-known missionaries of the Pacific area was John Paton. He knew that to take the gospel to the people of the New Hebrides was dangerous, but he understood the command of his Saviour, Jesus Christ - 'Go therefore and make disciples of all the nations' (Matthew 28:19). Despite the danger, he and his wife were settled on the island of Tanna where the natives were cannibals. Two of the first missionaries to the nearby island of Erromanga were John Williams and James Harris who were clubbed to death and eaten within a very short time of setting foot on the island.

John Paton and Mary, his young wife, were willing to sacrifice everything, even their lives, for the Lord Jesus. They knew his precious promise: 'Whoever desires to come after Me, let him deny himself, and take up his cross, and follow Me. For whoever desires to save his life will lose it, but whoever loses his life for My sake and the gospel's will save it. For what will it profit a man if he gains the whole world, and loses his own soul?' (Mark 8:34-36).

When John made the decision to become a missionary to the natives in the Pacific a man in his congregation warned him that he could well be killed and eaten by the cannibals. He replied, reminding the man that when he died, he would be buried and eaten by the worms. John told him plainly that he would rather be eaten by the natives than worms if it meant he was faithfully serving his Lord and Saviour, Jesus Christ.

John Paton suffered greatly for his Saviour. His wife, Mary, soon died on the island as did Peter, his little baby son.

What Christ is teaching is that we must be willing to make sacrifices when we become a Christian. But Jesus gave his people a special promise: 'I will never leave you nor forsake you.'

What sacrifices are you willing to make for Jesus?

The vicious natives made many efforts to drive John and several other missionaries from the island of Tanna. On one occasion their home was surrounded by the screaming natives, holding lighted torches and threatening to burn everything and kill them all. Without warning the cannibals became quiet and left the area. John Paton and his friends didn't know why this had happened until some time later when he spoke to the chief who had become a Christian: 'Why didn't your men burn us out and kill us all?' To this the chief replied: 'Who were all those armed men you had with you?'

When John said that he was there with just several other missionaries, the chief said when they had seen hundreds of big men standing near the mission station with shining swords in their hands they knew they had no hope in burning the missionary compound and killing the missionaries so they left.

John then knew that God had sent his angels to protect them from the murderous natives.

Angels are spirit beings, created by God to carry out his commands. One of their jobs is caring for God's people - even saving the lives of Christians when it is God's will. In the Bible you can read many stories of God's great angels protecting the saints. Read 2 Kings Chapter 19 where there is the story of God protecting Jerusalem from the Assyrian army. Read Acts 12:5-11 where God's angels saved Peter from the prison cells and escorted him to the safety of the house of Mary who was Mark's mother. God's promise in Psalm 34:7 is so true, 'The angel of the LORD encamps all around those who fear Him, and delivers them'. Often God's deliverance is to take his suffering people home to be with him.

God's angels protect the saints from Satan and his demons.

John Paton was eventually driven from the island of Tanna. After a trip to Great Britain, he married and returned to the New Hebrides where he settled on the less violent island of Aniwa. There he preached the gospel, but the natives showed little interest in God.

On Aniwa the witch doctors owned the only water hole and demanded payment for the scarce water. December to April was the rainy season and for the rest of the year fresh water was scarce. In the dry season the people usually drank coconut juice and washed themselves and their clothes in the salty ocean water. They only used fresh water for cooking and the occasional drink.

John had been preaching the wonderful gospel, urging the natives to repent of their sins and turn away from their witch doctors to the Lord Jesus. Of course most tribesmen feared the witch doctors who threatened death to anyone who turned to the God of the missionaries. John decided to break the power of the witch doctors once and for all.

He announced to the natives that he was going to sink a well and obtain fresh water. John told the people of Aniwa that his God supplied all their needs - even fresh water. John knew the words of Jeremiah 14:22 'Do any of the worthless idols of the nations bring rain? Do the skies themselves send down showers? No, it is you, O LORD our God. Therefore our hope is in you, for you are the one who does all this' (NIV). The faithful missionary had spent much time in prayer asking God to direct him to the spot where a well would be successful. God did not fail him.

When he announced his plan to the natives they thought he was mad and mocked his plans to find fresh water. Despite all the mocking and disbelief John began digging. The natives gathered about and watched what he was doing. Sometimes the sandy walls of the hole collapsed and the old chief Namakei pleaded with him to stop the work. He didn't believe fresh water could come from the ground, and he feared that John might be suffocated if the wall collapsed while he was in the well digging.

John kept working, always praying that God would produce fresh water from that hole. Then John announced that during the next day God would provide water from the ground. He had prayed that God would give the water which would be the way of showing the natives that Jehovah was the living God.

The following day the natives crowded about the well and after removing several more shovels full of sand the clear fresh water began to bubble up through the sand. Chief Namakei then said, 'From this day I believe that all he tells us about his Jehovah God is true. Today we have seen rain from the earth.'

He went on, 'In my heart I know that Jehovah does exist - the invisible God... I, your chief, do now firmly believe that when I die I shall see the invisible Jehovah God... From this day, my people and I must worship the God who has opened for us the well, and who fills us with rain from below. The gods of Aniwa cannot hear, cannot help us, like the God of Missi. Henceforth I am a follower of Jehovah God.'

At once the chief and some of his people came to John with their idols to have them destroyed.

From that day chief Namakei and many of his tribe became believers in the Lord Jesus Christ. A place was built for worship and in the years to come almost every member of the tribe confessed faith in Jesus. They knew the truth of Paul's words, 'Believe on the Lord Jesus Christ and you will be saved.'

Pirates

I'm sure you have heard about the fearsome English pirate, Blackbeard, who sailed the Caribbean Seas attacking ships, killing their crews and stealing all the treasure he could. He was born in 1680 and was killed in a battle with a British warship in 1718. He stole huge amounts of treasure, much of which was buried at places known only to a few members of the crew. If you have ever read the book *Treasure Island* by Robert Louis Stevenson you will find the fearsome Blackbeard mentioned several times.

Most pirates operated in the Atlantic Ocean attacking ships loaded with gold and other treasures. These ships were taking the treasures of America back to the rulers of powerful European countries. They were violent, cruel men who killed and murdered many innocent people. They laughed at God's law and showed no fear of those sent out to capture them and bring them to trial. Swords and guns hung from their waist. All pirates were proud of the many scars on their bodies, as they believed this was proof of their courage and fighting skills.

Some pirates sailed the Pacific Ocean along the coast of America attacking ships and then burying their treasures on deserted islands off the coast of South America. I'm sure that there is still a lot of undiscovered pirate treasure hidden on some Pacific islands.

Other buccaneers were to be found along the coast of Asia, many from China. These violent, cruel men terrorised the people along the western edge of the Pacific Ocean and stole huge amounts of money from the ships sent to buy spices from the East.

One very cruel pirate was Ching Shih whose husband, Zheng Yi, was a feared cutthroat pirate. He had a fleet of ships that he used

to attack British trading ships. When Zheng died Ching became

commander of about 1,500 pirate junks who plundered ships trading

with the 'East.' They were known to have invaded coastal towns

where they took prisoners, food and treasures. The fleet was known

as 'The Red Flag Fleet.'

The junks had sails but were often rowed. They carried cannons

that were used to capture the trading ships they wanted to board.

Some even had small rowing boats with light guns that allowed them

to get close to the trading ships. The guns on those bigger ships

couldn't be aimed down low.

Ching was a very cruel woman and was known to kill any sailor who disobeyed her commands. On one occasion a captive who was about to be whipped had his feet nailed to the junk's deck to make sure he couldn't escape. After this terrible punishment the poor man was put to death.

Chinese pirates frequently beheaded the people they captured, and after allowing the skulls to dry, hung them around their necks.

Now God's commandment is very plain for each one of us.

'You shall not murder' and 'You shall not steal' (Exodus 20:13,15).

Paul explained how we are to behave with each other - 'as we have opportunity, let us do good to all people, especially to those who belong to the family of believers' (Galatians 6:10 NIV). May you never be cruel to other people, but show kindness, compassion and Christian love.

War!

War is a terrible sin. People are killed and injured, property is destroyed, children lose parents and parents lose their children. During the 2nd World War there were many great battles fought in the Pacific Ocean. Some of you may have had relatives who were at Pearl Harbour in Hawaii on the day the Japanese attacked the American fleet.

It was on a lovely, peaceful Sunday morning - 7 December 1941 - when suddenly 180 Japanese planes dived out of the clouds to drop bombs and torpedoes on the ships in the harbour. The leader of the attacking planes was the great Japanese hero and pilot, Mitsuo

Fuchida. He was the one who gave the final order to his pilots at 7:49 am on that Lord's day morning, 'All squadrons plunge in to attack!' Then came the cry, 'Tora! Tora! Tora!' - 'Tiger! Tiger! Tiger!' After three hours of continual attacking more than 5,000 sailors and soldiers were dead and many more injured. Many citizens living in the area had also been killed. Eight American battleships were hit and only three were later able to sail again. Other ships were destroyed and the naval base was in ruins. Smoke filled the beautiful blue sky as the Japanese planes returned to their aircraft carriers.

Japan was now at war with the United States of America and when Mitsuo saw what a great success his warplanes had made he was overjoyed.

He was the son of a schoolteacher and was taught to hate Christianity and especially the American people. He had studied hard and eventually became a leader of the Japanese air force. Not only did he lead the attack on Pearl Harbour but he also lead the planes that bombed Darwin in Australia.

He said he would never surrender to the American army, but when the Japanese Emperor gave the order to surrender, he lay down his weapons and returned to a small farm where he grew crops to provide food for his family.

His hatred of the United States of America and Christianity grew, but one day when he was in Tokyo he was handed a tract about Jacob DeShazer who had become a Christian while in a Japanese prison of war camp in China. Instead of hating the Japanese Jacob now loved all people, even the cruel Japanese prison guards. After the war he had returned to Japan to tell the people about Jesus Christ, God's Son who had died on a Roman cross to pay the penalty for the sins of his people.

After reading DeShazer's story Mitsuo bought a Bible and on 14 April 1950 became a Christian. The Holy Spirit had changed his heart and now he loved Jesus Christ and all people, even the Americans whom he once hated and killed during the war. He then spent the rest of his life telling people about Jesus Christ his Saviour and inviting sinners to trust Him and love God - the God and Father of his Lord. Now Mitsuo told people that the only hope for this sinful and troubled world was Jesus Christ, his Saviour. He knew that the hatred people had for one another could never be removed without help from Jesus.

Now my young readers, what about you? Do you love God and are you trusting in Jesus Christ for your salvation? Have you repented of your sins? I trust this is true of each one of you. Without saving faith in the Lord Jesus you will never be allowed to enter heaven, but will forever be in hell, the place of everlasting punishment.

May God save you!

Beware of the Sharks

When my wife and I visited the USA early this century we visited the studio that produced the film - JAWS. We were taken on a boat ride where we saw the sets where many films had been made. Suddenly at one spot the huge face of a shark burst out of the water right beside our boat. It was very frightening to see the wide-open mouth filled with razor sharp, white teeth.

In all of the world's oceans we find sharks. The Pacific Ocean is known for some very huge ones - one being the Great White. This shark gained its name from its white belly and it has been reported that it grows to almost 9 metres in length - now that's big! The top part is grey in colour, which is a good camouflage. The Great White is considered the most dangerous shark in the world. Occasionally in Australia there is a report of someone being attacked by this huge creature and most victims die. The Great White doesn't like human flesh, but the terrible injuries from their bite causes bleeding that usually result in the death of the victim. These sharks feast on other sharks, dolphins, whales and fish. Their special delicacy is the seal.

The Great White frequently moves to the warmer ocean waters in winter, where they give birth to seven or eight live babies. These young ones are over a metre in length at birth and live about twenty-five years. Gradually their numbers are growing smaller and some people fear that they might die out.

This shark has six rows of razor sharp teeth, which grow to about eight centimetres in length. When our teeth wear out we have them repaired by the dentist and some of us wear a set of false teeth so that we can eat our food. God shows great wisdom with the replacement of a shark's teeth when one is broken off. They have rows of teeth and when a front tooth is broken off, the one behind gradually moves forward to fill the gap.

Now the Bible mentions teeth many times. In Psalm 57:4 we read of the psalmist's enemies - they were 'men whose teeth are spears and arrows.' This was to describe the cruel, hurtful way the ungodly treated God's people.

We read in the Psalmist's prayer: 'Break the teeth in their mouths, O God' (Psalm 58:6 NIV). Of course he wasn't really asking God to smash the teeth of the wicked, but to prevent those cruel, wicked people from hurting those who believed in God. He wanted God to make them weak like a toothless lion.

God created a great variety of sharks. There are many different sharks found in the world's oceans. On the most popular beaches lifesavers sound a loud siren when a shark is sighted in the waves. However, sharks are just another animal in God's creation. They are fearsome creatures, but once again show the genius of our Creator God.

Whales

Having read about the vicious sharks that kill their prey and make people very watchful when they go swimming, you are now going to read about the gentle giants of the Pacific Ocean - the whales! The Pacific Ocean is well known for the very large whales that live in its waters. They are the largest mammals found in the world and the Blue Whale grows to over one hundred tons. Today most people complain very loudly when they hear that these graceful, friendly mammals are hunted and killed. Once they were killed for their oil to be used in lamps, but today there is no reason why these loveable creatures of the ocean should be slaughtered.

A whale is a mammal. This means it is warm blooded, just like you and me. It gives birth to a fully developed youngster that stays with its mother for about a year, drinking milk from her teat. It lives in the water but breathes air. This means that it takes a big breath of air and then dives below the surface of the ocean searching for food. When it surfaces to get another breath it appears that a spurt of water comes from the hole in its head. Really all that happens is that warm air is blown into the cool air and small droplets of water are formed. In the distance this 'steam' looks like a gush of water.

If you visit a Pacific island I'm sure you will have the opportunity to travel out to sea on a whale watching expedition. Many whales are friendly and move close to the boats where they splash about as if 'showing off' to the watching humans.

Whales have an underwater noise language by which they 'speak' to one another. Many whales spend the summer months in the cold Polar waters such as Antarctica where they feast upon the great schools of krill - small prawn like creatures. While in that region they put on weight, which helps keep them warm in the freezing water and builds up a supply of energy that they need in the winter months.

As winter approaches the whales travel north to the warm waters of the Pacific Ocean where they give birth to their young. The Humpback and Southern Right Whales usually follow the same route each year and many watchers along the Australian coast recognize whales that have travelled that way many times.

One interesting whale that nearly became extinct because of its slaughter is the Southern Right Whale. These gentle creatures are slow moving and the early whale hunters claimed these were the 'Right' ones to hunt. When harpooned and dead they floated to the surface making it easy to haul them onto the large whaling ships.

Another well-known whale is the Killer Whale - Orca. They are very intelligent and often hunt in packs. They have been known to take revenge on another animal that has hurt them or their lifelong mate.

Again whales display the wonder of God's creation. Some people think that Jonah was swallowed by a whale. The Bible tells us that when Jonah was thrown overboard by the terrified sailors the LORD 'prepared a great fish to swallow Jonah. And Jonah was in the belly of the fish three days and three nights' (Jonah 1:17).

Maybe it was a whale that swallowed Jonah. I read a story of a whale hunter being swallowed alive by a whale. In 1931 when he was on a whaling expedition he fell into the water after his boat had been smashed by its tail. The next thing he knew, he was sliding down a dark passage. Realizing that he was inside a whale, his terror mounted and he became unconscious. Two days later, as the whale was being cut up after capture, the man was found in its stomach. After some slight medical attention, he was brought to consciousness and normal health. His skin had suffered from the acids in the whale's stomach, but apart from that he was completely unhurt.*

I don't think that man would have gone whaling any more - would you after such a frightening experience? Take your time and read the story of Jonah. He was taught that he had to obey God's commands. We must always do the same, but our reason for obedience must be that we love Jesus Christ, the Saviour and law giver. Is Jesus your Lord and Saviour?

Science returns to God, by James Jauncey, Zondervan Publishing House, Grand Rapids, 1963, p. 81.

Easter Island

Easter Island is a very remote and small island - 3,600 kilometres from the coast of Chile and only 170 square kilometres in size. Like most Pacific islands it is the tip of three huge volcanoes. The natives called their homeland 'Te Pito o Tehenau' which means 'The navel of the world.'

The first European to visit the island was the Dutchman, Jacob Roggeveen, who arrived there on Easter Sunday, 5 April 1772. You now know the reason for the name 'Easter Island.'

This isolated island is a land of mysteries. It was settled by Polynesians several hundred years after the birth of Jesus. It was a fertile land with trees, especially palms, but when the European explorers arrived they found an island without trees and populated by natives living in caves and homes made of reeds. There was little food available for the people, who lived on yams and chickens. Obviously the Polynesian settlers had brought hens and roosters with them when they arrived on their large twin hulled sailing boats. The platform between the two hulls had space for the people on board, animals, plants and everything else the settlers would need to make life easy in their new land.

There is no coral reef surrounding Easter Island. This means that fish are not very plentiful. Indeed there were very few creatures on this new homeland, just some insects and lizards.

When the Polynesians settled on their new homeland the land produced crops and a great civilisation grew. What happened after that no one is sure, but the island gradually became very bare. The trees were gone and natives had little food. Some were also cannibals.

On the island the explorers discovered more than 300 great stone platforms called 'Ahu.' They were probably used for worship and the burial of the native chiefs. At each Ahu and surrounding the island were great stone carvings of a man's head and body. These were called 'Moai' and were very weighty. Many had great blocks of stone - 'Topnots' - resting on their head.

The stone for these monuments had been dragged from the quarries of the Rano Raraku volcano. It would have taken between

sixty and 150 natives to drag the stones into place. To make possible the moving of the heavy rock slabs it was believed that they were dragged across tree trunks. Perhaps this was the reason for the Palm trees on Easter Island being cut down.

The work of carving the statues came to an end and some partly finished ones were left lying about the quarry. Legend tells us that war broke out between the two great tribes - the 'Long Ears' who had made the great statues and the 'Short Ears.' The Short ears won

the battle, but they were left with a bare island with few trees and little food. They were unable to build boats for fishing or homes to live in. The only source of fresh water was in the small lakes near the volcano. Life was very hard for the inhabitants of Easter Island. They had destroyed their island.

I think that we are doing the same to our world. Great areas are ruined because trees have been cut down. Rivers are poisoned by chemicals and many animals and plants have become extinct. God didn't create this world for us to destroy. Indeed God told Adam to care for it. We read: '...the LORD God took the man and put him in the garden of Eden to tend and keep it' (Genesis 2:15).

Let each one of us do all we can to preserve this wonderful world. Sin has caused great harm to both humans and the rest of creation. Paul wrote that a better day was coming '... the creation itself also will be delivered from the bondage of corruption' (Romans 8:21). This will happen when our Saviour returns and makes the new heavens and earth that will be perfect in every way.

Fiji

These days many newly wed couples spend their honeymoon in Fiji, which is one of the most beautiful spots in the Pacific. It is hard to believe that the ancestors of these friendly people were once fearsome cannibals, who after killing their enemies, cooked and ate their bodies.

Most of the 330 islands that make up the nation of Fiji are volcanic in origin, but over the centuries the tiny polyps have been hard at work building their colourful coral homes, which form reefs about the islands. The result is golden, sandy beaches and clear, blue ocean water teeming with a multitude of brightly coloured fish swimming and feeding amongst the outcrops of coral. It is really an undersea wonderland.

Suva, the capital city of Fiji is situated on the island of Viti Leve. From the word 'Viti' comes the name 'Fiji.' 'Fiji' is simply the way the natives pronounced the island's name. Originally it was

pronounced 'Fisi' but with the passing of generations the name became 'Fiji.'

The main products of the nation are sugar, coconuts, cotton, gold and cloth. In the early days one Fijian product that was very popular in Great Britain was the brightly coloured cloth that was used to make sarongs.

While most people live a simple agricultural life style,

thousands are employed in the tourist industry. Many islands have hotels and bungalows for the many tourists who enjoy the pleasantly warm climate.

And there is so much for visitors to see and do. There are 126 different bird species, most of which are very brightly coloured. The countryside has over 3,000 different species of plants and of this number more than 1,000 have flowers. One of the most beautiful walkways is through the Abaca Cultural and Recreational Park where a multitude of birds can be seen flying about the brightly coloured trees and shrubs in the rain forest. This particular walk passes some spectacular waterfalls. Fiji has very few native animals. There are three mammals - a native rat and two types of bats. As well there are only seven reptiles and amphibians native to the islands.

Not far from Suva is Fiji's tallest mountain – Tomanivi. It is really an extinct volcano, 1,323 metres high.

The first Europeans to visit Fiji were the Dutch explorers, the best-known being Abel Tasman, after whom the Tasman Sea

was named. He visited Fiji in 1643, but avoided the natives when he learned that they were cannibals. Later Captain James Cook made contact with the natives and soon after in the early nineteenth century missionaries and traders settled there. In 1874 Britain claimed the Fijian people and islands as a colony, and it was not until 1970 that the nation became an independent democracy.

In the early colonial days the British established sugar, cotton and coconut plantations, but at first this was not very successful as the Fijians were used to an easy way of life - not the hard work on plantations. As a result the British brought thousands of Indians to do the work that the Fijians didn't want. These people were very hard workers and were happy to make Fiji their new home. Many became wealthy, buying land and opening shops.

To the native Fijians it seemed that the Indians were taking over their country. When independence was granted, all citizens were given the right to vote and soon people, descended from the original Indian settlers, gained seats in the parliament. This caused a lot of ill feeling. The leaders of the Fijian army overthrew the government on two occasions - 1987 and 2000. They weren't going to have a Prime Minister of Indian descent ruling their country.

Even though the Indian citizens of Fiji make up almost half of the population of about 1,000,000, laws have been passed preventing land being owned by Fijians of Indian descent.

These coups had a disastrous effect upon the tourist trade as few people wanted to visit a nation which was ruled by the army. As a result many workers lost their jobs, but now all seems settled and tourists are again returning to that beautiful country.

Following the great spiritual revivals in Great Britain, Christian missionaries spread out throughout the world telling people about the salvation that was to be found in the Lord Jesus Christ.

God greatly blessed the work of the missionaries in Fiji and many people became Christians. They realised all men and women are made in the image of God and that to kill and eat another person is a terrible sin. The natives began to understand the wickedness of sin and the holiness of God. They understood that God demanded all people to obey His law and live in peace with each other. In the 1996 census 97 percent of the Fijians claimed to be Christians, most being members of the original Methodist Church.

The Lord's day is still precious to them and each Sunday shops are closed and most people attend worship. The singing of psalms and hymns is glorious to hear as the Fijian people have the natural ability not only to sing sweetly but to sing in harmony. The influence of Christianity is seen in the Fijian national anthem which is 'God bless Fiji.' The country's motto is 'Fear God and honour the Queen.'

Despite the claim of most people to be Christians the Fijians are divided on the basis of race. The native Fijians believe those of Indian descent are taking over their country. This is very sad!

When Jesus walked the earth the Jews, who knew they were God's chosen people, despised the Samaritans and Gentiles. However, when Jesus was asked what was the greatest commandment He replied, "'You shall love the LORD your God with all your heart, with all your soul, and with all your mind.' This is the first and great commandment. And the second is like it: 'You shall love your neighbour as yourself'" (Matthew 22:37-39). Jesus then told the parable of the Good Samaritan in which he pointed out that we are all neighbours to one another (Luke 10:29-37).

In the early Christian church the Christian Jews and Gentiles sat side by side to worship God and thank Jesus for His work of salvation. Paul wrote that the Christians were one in Christ and that Jesus had broken down the wall of hatred between the two groups of people.

Many sports are played by the Fijians, but the most popular are Rugby Union and League. Fijian teams play in world competitions and several times their team has become world champions.

Unfortunately education is not compulsory in Fiji. Free education is available to all young people, but parents must pay for higher schooling. As a result only about 90 percent of the population can read and write. Reading is a very important skill for everyone. If you cannot read, you can't study your Bible. If you can read and have your own Bible, thank God for such wonderful gifts.

Despite the changes made since the country became a British colony, much remains the same. In Suva the tallest building is only fourteen storeys tall.

Maybe one day you will have a holiday in Fiji where the green countryside is dotted with many brightly coloured flowers and birds. You will enjoy the golden sands on the beaches. Most tourists spend time swimming, surfing, diving and snorkelling. Others try their hand at fishing and usually return with a good catch. Some spend time sailing about the many islands, enjoying the beautiful scenery and lazing in the warm tropical climate.

Fiji is a great holiday destination.

Hawaii

The waves that roll across the wide Pacific ocean to the surf beaches of Australia have travelled all the way from Hawaii. One water sport I often wish I had undertaken when I was young is surfboard riding. It seems to be such a great sport, riding the big waves as they crash onto the beach. I tried several times, but was a complete failure. I kept falling off the surfboard! However, even though I can't ride a surfboard I very much enjoy sitting on the sandy beach and watching the energetic young people enjoying their sport - especially when the waves are big! It is possibly the best place in the world for surfboard riders.

Hawaii is the 50th state of the United States of America, the only state not attached to the mainland. and about 3,900 kilometres from the shores of North America. It is not just one island, but a row of over 100 islands, many of which are uninhabited. The island state is called Hawaii because that is the name of - 'the Big Island.' The eight larger islands are very popular with tourists who visit the tropical paradise.

The Hawaiian islands are really the tops of great volcanoes rising up from the seabed. These islands have been beautified by

the millions of tiny polyps working hard to build their coral homes. The results are coral reefs of a great variety of shapes and colours. They have become the homes for the many different fish that live and feed amongst them.

The clear blue water, sandy beaches, the underwater coloured wonderland, the warm climate and friendly people make Hawaii a very popular tourist destination. The climate is pleasant all the year round due to the 'trade winds' that constantly waft across the ocean.

The capital city is Honolulu which is situated on the island of Oahu. It fronts Waikiki which is one of the best beaches in the world. Those who enjoy the surf travel to Waimea Bay as it is there that some of the biggest and best waves can be found. The ocean swells sweep across the deep Pacific and suddenly reach the shallow waters about the Hawaiian islands. This causes waves to rise high and thunder down on the beaches. The seabed at Waimea Bay causes waves, some ten metres tall, to crash on the coral reef beside the beach. These huge waves are the great attraction to surfboard riders, but they can be quite dangerous as well. If a surfer falls from his board it could mean a lengthy underwater stay, as well as the danger of being smashed onto the razor sharp coral.

This region is the most popular tourist destination in Hawaii.

The island of Oahu is well known for the American navy base established in 1908. This naval establishment at Pearl Harbour was attacked by the Japanese air force on 7 December 1941, with the result that the United States of America became involved in

World War II. Today Pearl Harbour is still a naval base, but is also a memorial for the many courageous men and women who lost their lives in that Japanese bombing raid.

The island of Hawaii still has active volcanoes, the best known being Loa and Kilauea. Lava, smoke and ash frequently are belched from the crater of these huge volcanoes and often a river of sparkling red hot lava creeps down the slopes and into the surrounding ocean water. Boiling lava has been known to travel at about twenty kilometres per hour and to move as far as twenty kilometres before it becomes solid. When the lava reaches the ocean, the water boils, creating a spectacular sight for visitors. These volcanoes are continually adding to the size of the island. Deep down on the seabed there are active volcanoes pouring out red hot lava, and if the world lasts long enough this will eventually make new islands.

Yet close to this volcanic region on the island of Hawaii is the Kau Desert which is beside dense rain forests. This region is a desert formed by volcanic ash where nothing grows. Hawaii is really a land of contrasts.

Before Christianity was brought to the native people it was believed that the god 'Pele' was the cause of the eruption of the volcanoes. The people believed each eruption was caused when Pele became angry. Some claim to have seen Pele swimming in the red hot lava and even today there is a saying, 'Watch out for old ladies: one of them may be Pele!'

Soon after missionaries settled in Hawaii a chieftainess, Kapiolani, decided to stand up against Pele. It was believed that before anyone could eat the lovely 'ohelo' berries, some had to be thrown into or towards a boiling lava pit. The natives believed that those berries were the property of Pele. To eat them before offering some to her would mean death by incineration. When Kapiolani commenced eating the berries without making the necessary offering to Pele, a priestess from one of Pele's temples showed her a letter of warning supposedly written by Pele. To this Kapiolani replied, 'I also have a letter. Jehovah is my God. He lit these fires. I don't fear Pele. If I am killed now by Pele then you should fear your god. But I trust Jehovah, and He will keep me safe from Pele's anger...'

Kapiolani thought she had a copy of the Bible in her hand, which she said was her letter from Jehovah, but really it was a spelling book which she had been given to help her learn to read English. She threw what she thought was the Bible into the volcanic lava and Pele failed to hurt her. The power of Pele was broken!

Let us remember that there is one God who said to the Israelites - and to us as well: 'You shall have no other gods before Me'

(Exodus 20:3). Also remember what Jesus said was the first and greatest commandment: 'You shall love the LORD your God with all your heart, with all your soul, and with all your mind' (Matthew 22:37). Do you love God as Jesus commanded?

Eruptions are spectacular sights in Hawaii, but the red hot lava destroys crops, roads and homes. It has been recorded that boiling lava has been thrown over 600 metres into the air.

In 1942 Mauna Loa erupted and the smoke, ash and red hot lava provided a guide for Japanese submarines searching for boats to attack and sink. During the night they could fix their position from the glow of the lava and during the daylight hours from the smoke rising high into the sky.

Some of Hawaii's most beautiful regions are found in the jungle regions about Mauna Loa. It is a region of dense rain forest, with some trees that started growing at the time when the Lord Jesus walked this earth - these trees are over 2,000 years old! In this rain forest there is a multitude of brightly coloured flowers and every shade of green. The beautiful Kamehameha butterflies are found here and they have wing spans of up to twelve centimetres.

The 'Ti' plant has proved of great value to the natives. Its leaves are used for roof covering, clothes and when some food is to be roasted, the meat is wrapped in the large leaves.

One unusual plant growing in Hawaii is the bright, grey Silversword. Every ten to fifteen years it grows a column about two metres tall and this is covered with maroon florets. This plant has bright fibreglass like hairs that reflect the hot sunlight during the day

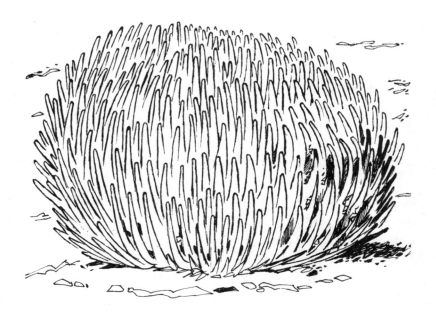

time and a growth at ground level which protects the roots during the freezing cold nights. Now, I'm sure this just didn't evolve, but rather shows the wisdom and almighty intelligence of God who created all things.

On Kauai Island there is the extinct volcano - Waialeale- which is known not just for the dense jungle region and the many spectacular waterfalls, but because it is the wettest place in the world, having an annual rainfall of 460 inches - 11,685 mm. In 1982 666 inches of rain (16,916 milimetres) were recorded. Strangely just a few miles away the annual rainfall is just 10 inches (250 milimetres) annually.

Because of its spectacular scenery this island has been used to make many films. Several best known ones were 'King Kong', 'Raiders of the Lost Ark', 'South Pacific' and 'Jurassic Park III.'

The Hawaiian natives were great warriors and many wars were fought between the tribes inhabiting the islands. The tribal chiefs were greatly feared and in one region if the shadow of the chief fell upon any member of the tribe, that person was immediately put to death. This meant that natives treated the chief with awe and respect. At feasting time, when the chief inhaled the smoke of the burning leaves of the Pukiane tree the taboo was lifted.

This should remind us that unforgiven sin means eternal death - hell. Our only protection comes from the Lord Jesus Christ who by his death on the cross paid the penalty owed by His people because of their sins. When He perfectly obeyed God's law he gave us His righteousness, making it possible for us to enter heaven. We have a glorious Saviour.

One of the greatest British explorers, Captain James Cook, was murdered in Hawaii. He was the first European to visit the Hawaiian

islands, naming them the 'Sandwich Islands' after John Montagu, the Earl of Sandwich, who at that time was the First Lord of the Admiralty. Cook was treated as a god by the natives, but when he was forced to return to Hawaii after damage to his ship in a storm, a dispute broke out between the sailors and the natives. The locals had stolen one of Cook's boats and he wanted it returned. The result of the argument was that Captain Cook was stabbed in the back and killed. This happened on 14 February, 1779.

Today a memorial stands on the shores of Kealakua Bay and in 1877 a small piece of land was given to the British Government. This means that there is a small piece of British territory in the 50th state of the USA.

Hawaii is truly a wonderland in the Pacific.

Tonga

Like the many islands of the Pacific, Tonga is found on the Pacific Ocean 'Ring of Fire' which is known for volcanoes and earthquakes. Most of the Tongan islands are extinct volcanoes that rose from the ocean floor to appear above sea level. In this region the ocean has a depth of ten kilometres - that's a long way down! Tonga consists of 171 islands, but only has an area of 718 square kilometres. The population live on forty-five of these islands and many work small farms and help care for the many tourists who visit Tonga.

Most of the islands are surrounded by coloured coral reefs which attract a multitude of fish that live and feed there.

Some of the islands still have active volcanoes which are spectacular when they erupt. Today, Tofua volcano frequently belches out fire, smoke, ash and brimstone. Occasionally new islands appear as a movement of the ocean floor causes the tops of volcanoes to break through the surface of the ocean. In 1995 a new island appeared and was named Metis Shoal. Just as new islands appear, so also small islands sink below the ocean surface.

The Tongans were once cannibals but missionaries visited the islands and in 1831 King George Tupou became a Christian. As a result most citizens followed their King and began to trust in the Lord Jesus Christ. Sunday - the Lord's Day - is very special to the people today. All shops are closed and most people walk to worship, dressed in their best clothes. Ordinary work is forbidden. Isn't it sad that in our countries most people use the Lord's Day for anything but the worship of the living God?

The Tongans are very friendly people, and when Captain James Cook visited the islands he called them 'The Friendly Islands.'

Children respect their elders and the King is treated with special honour. When the King passes along the roadway in his car, as a sign of respect the citizens sit down and remain seated until he is out of sight.

The Tongans once hunted whales and the first kill of the season was given to the King. This reminds us of the law of God which demanded that the firstfruits of the harvest be presented to the priests. The first of the animals also belonged to the Lord. When the Israelites invaded the Promised Land, Joshua told the people that everything from the city of Jericho, the first city to be attacked, was to be devoted to God. These treasures were to be placed in the tabernacle and used to meet the costs of God's house.

However, Achan stole clothes and treasure from Jericho and was put to death for that terrible sin. You and I have to support the work of the gospel so make sure you put aside a part of your pocket money for the Lord's work.

Flying Foxes are the only native mammals found on the islands. They were considered to be sacred and could only be hunted by the royal family.

One game the children play is Pani. Maybe you could get your friends to join you in this game.

You need a tennis ball, some tin cans and two teams of possibly more than 3 players in each team. The first team has to build a tower with their tins, but while working the other team throws their ball to knock down the tower. If a member of the building team is hit by the ball they must leave the area. This could be shown by drawing a

very big circle and those throwing the balls were not to step into the circle, except to get their ball. As the tower is built the team counts out aloud the number of tins packed on one another. When 10 tins are piled up they call out 'Pani' and are awarded one point.

When all members of the side are out, the other team goes in. You can set the number of innings for a game and the team with the greatest number of points is the winner.

Whenever a ball or stone is thrown I think of David, the shepherd boy who bravely faced Goliath, the great Philistine warrior. Everyone feared Goliath except David who spoke to King Saul: 'Your servant

71

has killed both lion and bear; and this uncircumcised Philistine will be like one of them, seeing he has defied the armies of the living God.... The LORD, who delivered me from the paw of the lion and from the paw of the bear, He will deliver me from the hand of this Philistine' (1 Samuel 17:36-37).

Using his sling he threw the stone at Goliath and killed him. David was a good shot, but God was with him to give him courage to face Goliath. It is a terrible sin to ridicule the living God and turn your back on the Lord Jesus Christ.

The Cook Islands

There are only fifteen islands that make up the 'Cook Islands' and they cover just 241 square kilometres of land. The capital city, Avarua, is found on the island of Rarotonga. Again the islands are just the tops of huge underwater volcanoes about which the polyps have built their coral homes. The Cook islands were named after the great British explorer, Captain James Cook.

In the 1820s missionaries came to the islands and after teaching the people about Christ the Saviour, many natives came to trust their lives to Jesus. The best known missionary on the islands was Rev John Williams of the London Missionary Society. God blessed the work of the missionaries and cannibalism came to an end when the people were converted. Sunday is still precious to the people of the Cook islands and there are strict laws to enforce the people to keep the Lord's Day holy. Indeed there are fines for anyone who fails to obey the laws of Sunday observance.

Sadly, the coming of white people also brought their diseases with the result that 70 percent of the natives in the area died.

The Cook islands, being so isolated have only one native animal and that is the fruit bat.

The countryside is beautiful. The rain forests are filled with a variety of ferns and colourful plants, especially the beautiful Hibiscus. These bright flowers are worn in the hair and the plants are used to make skirts, ropes and sandals. The branches are used to make the walls of their homes and from the flowers the natives make medicine.

Along the cliffs of Atiu island there are many limestone caves. In a cave named Anataketake lives the indigenous bird - the Kopeka.

These small birds fly about in the dark without bumping into one another, the walls or the stalactites as they are guided by the echoes of their clicking sounds.

There is an abundance of wonderfully coloured birds living on the Cook Islands and one recently saved from extinction is the small Rarotonga flycatcher. In 1989 this bird was one of the ten rarest birds in the world. Only twenty-nine were known to be alive, but with care and a special breeding program their numbers have increased.

Ten pairs of these birds were placed on the island of Atiu and it appears that this little bird which grows to just fourteen centemetres has been saved from extinction. Their greatest enemies are rats and cats that Europeans have brought to the islands.

The waters surrounding the Cook islands are a wonderland for visitors who enjoy watching the whales. During August and September Humpback whales return to this area to breed before swimming down to the cold Antarctic waters to feed. On the beaches you would find a multitude of crabs. In fact it is recorded that there are at least 200 different species of crabs on the islands.

If you visited the Cook islands you would have a lot to do and see. There are walkways through the dense rain forests and the coral reef. You can also go snorkelling and have a close look at the coloured coral and fish. Many people enjoy a trip in a glass bottomed boat in order to see the coloured wonderland under the ocean surface. The Cook islands are a lovely part of the Pacific Ocean.

Samoa and Bora Bora

Like the majority of the Pacific islands, Samoa is made up of volcano tops poking their heads through the ocean waters. Samoa has two main islands - Savai'i and Upolu that are surrounded by coral reefs which add to their beauty.

They form a tropical paradise with coloured coral, fish, birds and trees and shrubs. The beaches are covered with a pure white sand and tourists enjoy walking through the dense rain forests on tracks which lead to spectacular waterfalls. The natives sell coffee, bananas, cocoa, timber and fish, especially tuna.

Many of the volcanic islands in the Pacific rise high into the sky, but some are just a few feet above sea level. It is believed that if global warming is true some very low level Samoan islands will be first to be submerged by the rising ocean level.

A popular sport played in Samoa is Kirikiti. It is a strange

version of cricket, but played very seriously and with different rules. The bat has three sides which means no one can be sure in which direction the rubber ball, coated with pandanus, will go when it is hit. Because the ball is not round in shape, it bounces in any direction. In one area scoring is as follows

- if the ball hits the boundary - a fence, a row of houses, the front gardens or the church - the batter scores one point. If the ball goes beyond the boundary the batter is given two points. If the ball is hit into the coconut plantation it is a four and if the ball is lost it counts as six.

Usually the teams are twenty two in number, but this rule is changed to make sure everyone is involved. So serious is the game that arguments have resulted in a person's death. You can check the rules from the internet and maybe start a game of Kirikiti in your backyard. Just make up your own rules as it seems that any rules are permitted.

It is recorded that 99 percent of the Samoan people are Christians. Sunday - the Lord's day - is kept holy and most people attend worship. Another interesting fact is that at 6:30 pm every day of the week the island bell is rung. This is a reminder that it is time for evening prayer. Do you have family worship in your home? Some Christian families gather together in their homes each day for a time of worship. The Scriptures are read, prayer is made to the living God and songs of praise are sung. It is sad that today very few parents gather their children about the Word of God to daily worship the Lord Jesus Christ. If this doesn't happen in your home, then perhaps you could ask your Mum or Dad if they would start 'family worship.'

God gave the Israelites His perfect law which the people were to obey. One of these laws involved parents teaching their children about the living God. Moses wrote God's instructions: 'Fix these words of mine in your hearts and minds ... Teach them to your children, talking about them when you sit at home and when you walk along the road, when you lie down and when you get up...' (Deuteronomy 11:18-21).

The Lord Jesus was known for the wonderful stories he told the people. They are called parables and each parable teaches something about God and His truth. Samoa was known for a man who was a wonderful story teller - Robert Louis Stevenson. He was given

the name 'Tusitala' - 'Teller of Tales.' This man came from Great

Britain because of sickness and made his home on the island of

Upolu. He knew that living in a different climate would help him

lead a more healthy and useful life. One of his books you should

read is 'Treasure Island'. Today his home is a museum.

The Lord Jesus told a story about a pearl. He said, 'The kingdom

of heaven is like a merchant seeking beautiful pearls, who, when he

had found one pearl of great price, went and sold all that he had and bought it' (Matthew 13:45, 46). He was saying that salvation and membership in the kingdom of heaven is of more value than a perfect pearl. The sinner's greatest need is met by the Lord Jesus Christ. He is precious and is 'the pearl of great price.'

One small island in the Pacific is named 'Bora Bora' - 'the First Born.' This island, because of its great beauty, has been called 'The Pearl of the Pacific.' It is part of the Society Islands, named by Captain Cook because the many islands were close together - they were to him a 'society of islands.'

Bora Bora is the top of several extinct volcanoes rising through the ocean and is surrounded by a beautiful coral reef. The volcanoes are named Mount Pahia which is 660 metres tall and Mount Otemanu which is 725 metres in height. These volcano tips, when surrounded by low clouds look very mysterious. Bora Bora in 2007 had a population of just less that 10,000 citizens. Many tourists visit the island each year to relax and enjoy the beauty of this 'Pearl' in the Pacific. Two smaller islands are nearby - Toopua and Toopuaiti.

Bora Bora has the most beautiful lagoon within the coral reef about the island. The coral makes the water appear to be a variety of blues in colour. The white, sandy beach is surrounded by rain forests dotted with a multitude of colours from the hibiscus shrubs that grow in great numbers.

The island was settled by Polynesians about 900 years after the birth of Jesus. They built stone temples and even today there remains carved idols of what they believed to be sacred turtles.

The island has been used as a set for several movies and during World War II the Americans established a base on the island from which they launched attacks upon the Japanese forces.

When you hear people speaking of Bora Bora we remember the writer, James Michiner who said that the island and its lagoon were 'so stunning, that there are no adequate words to describe it.'

Our Saviour, the Lord Jesus Christ, is perfect in every way. No words can be used to describe His glory. Jesus Christ is truly the 'Pearl without Price.'

A Volcano and an Island

In 1788, Henry Ball, the commander of *HMS Supply* came across a small tip of a volcano rising 550 metres into the sky. He named the rock after himself. *The Guinness Book of Records* claims it is the highest rock pinnacle in the world. However, it is gradually being torn apart by the huge swells sweeping across the Pacific Ocean. It has no harbours and for many years no one set foot on it. Some sailors tried to swim there but the fierce local birds and the fifteen centimetre centipedes caused them to quickly retreat to their boats.

The Bible speaks about a 'Rock' - the Lord Jesus. Peter wrote: 'Behold, I lay in Zion a chief cornerstone, elect, precious, and he who believes on Him will by no means be put to shame. Therefore, to you who believe, He is precious; but to those who are disobedient, "The stone which the builders rejected Has become the chief cornerstone" ...' (1 Peter 2:6,7). All who believe in the Lord Jesus will never suffer shame. The world might try and make us feel ashamed, but always remember what Jesus did for his people. He was mocked and put to shame so that all who trust in him might live forever in the home he has prepared for them.

Some years ago I spent a week on Norfolk Island. It is an isolated part of the Pacific and was discovered by Captain Cook in 1774. It is only a small piece of land eight kilometres by five kilometres with some parts rising 105 metres above sea

level. It became well known because of the tall pines growing on its hillsides. The islanders now plant a special pine tree in remembrance of all people who live to be 100 years old.

This lovely island was not always a pleasant place, as it was once a penal colony. First, twenty-two convicts were sent from Sydney to Norfolk to farm the rich soil and produce food for those living at the Sydney settlement. Even though it is 1,400 kilometres from Australia the farms provided much needed food for soldiers and convicts back in Sydney.

The colony was closed in 1814, but reopened later to house the worst convicts. The soldiers on guard treated the prisoners with great cruelty. On one occasion a group of convicts was sentenced to death by hanging, only to find out later that several were to be reprieved. Those who escaped the gallows broke down - weeping and pleading that they also might be hung, so hard was life on Norfolk.

During the second time that Norfolk was used to house convicts, stone buildings were erected - prisons, homes and a hospital. This time there were over 2,000 soldiers and convicts living there.

Sin is a terrible thing. We are born sinners and so easily break God's commands. God told Adam and Eve they would be punished if they broke His law. We know they did so and we know also God's word: 'The wages of sin is death' (Romans 6:23). This death is both the death of our body and spiritual death. The only way to escape hell is to trust Jesus Christ who suffered in the place of his people. He died that His people might live forever.

The poor convicts on Norfolk Island suffered cruel punishment for breaking the laws of Great Britain and Australia. It is sad to read the tombstones on this island. Many of the people who died here were young.

When Norfolk was closed down as a penal colony most convicts were sent to Tasmania where conditions were almost as cruel. Today the relics of the convict days are there for all to see, but it is a pleasant place for a holiday.

The Mutiny on the Bounty

On 23 December 1787 *HMS Bounty* sailed from England, commanded by William Bligh. The ship was to visit Tahiti to gather eggfruit plants. These were to be taken to the West Indies and the vegetable used to feed slaves. Bligh had a bad temper and when he was angry cursed and swore at the crew. Because of this he became unpopular with the sailors. His good friend, Fletcher Christian, was second in charge of the ship.

Arriving at Tahiti, the crew had a pleasant six months gathering the plants and enjoying life with the natives. In fact life was so pleasant some of the crew wanted to remain on the island. On board the *Bounty* there were complaints about a lack of food, not enough space for exercise and disappointment at leaving such a lovely part of the world.

On 28 April 1789 a mutiny, led by Fletcher Christian took place and Bligh with thirty of his men were placed in the ship's small boat and left with food and water to save themselves. Those mutineers should have obeyed the command of God given by Paul: 'Be obedient to those who are your masters according to the flesh, with fear and trembling, in sincerity of heart, as to Christ' (Ephesians 6:5).

Bligh, who later became the Governor of the convict settlement at Sydney successfully sailed the boat 3,600 kilometres to Timor. This trip took forty-eight days without loss of any lives.

Fletcher Christian and his mutineers sailed to Pitcairn Island which was very isolated and only 4.6 square kilometres in size. They had some Polynesian men and women with them and began to treat them as slaves. When they wanted to return to their homeland

trouble broke out and some people were murdered. Eventually

only one of the mutineers survived. He was John Adams who had

been taught to read and prayerfully studied a Bible given to him

by a friend. He became a Christian and when he taught the rest of

the islanders about the Lord peace settled on the island. Sunday

services were held, but the island was not large enough for the

growing families.

Finally, the British Queen Victoria gave them Norfolk Island

as their home. Norfolk seemed to be a Paradise to them and each

family head was given twenty hectares of land. Some time later,

many of the settlers decided to return to Pitcairn Island leaving the

descendants of Fletcher Christian and the mutineers as the owners

of Norfolk Island, which they are to this very day.

Now the island is a tourist resort - a Paradise in the Pacific, but

not to be compared with God's Paradise - the new heavens and new

earth in which the saints will live when Jesus returns. Will you have

a place in God's paradise? You will if you are a Christian and trust

in your Lord and Saviour, Jesus Christ.

Quiz

1. What nationality was the explorer Ferdinand Magellan?

2. How many times bigger than the USA is the Pacific Ocean?

3. In Isaiah 40:12 what does God measure in his hand?

4. How many days did God take to create the world?

5. What islands did Charles Darwin visit in 1835?

6. Name the missionary who went to the New Hebrides?

7. Who was Ching Shih?

8. What is a junk?

9. In what chapter in Exodus do we find the ten commandments?

10. Where is Pearl Harbour?

11. What did Mitsuo Fuchido do during World War II?

12. How many rows of teeth does a Great White shark have?

13. What body part does David use to describe his enemies in Psalm 57:4?

14. Is a whale a fish or a mammal?

15. Where do whales spend the summer months?

16. How did Easter Island get its name?

17. What has God told us to do with the world in Genesis 2:15?

18. What are the five main products of Fiji?

19. What was the island of Fiji originally called?

20. What nation does Hawaii belong to?

21. What are Loa and Kilauea?

22. What are the only native mammals found on Tonga?

23. What missionary visited the Cook Islands during the 1800s?

24. How many species of crab live on the Cook Islands?

25. Bora Bora has two other names. What are they?

26. Who is truly the pearl without price?

27. Who led the Mutiny on the *Bounty*?

Answers

1. Portuguese

2. Seventeen times bigger.

3. The waters

4. Six

5. The Galapagos Islands

6. John Paton

7. A Chinese female pirate.

8. A small boat

9. Exodus 20

10. Hawaii

11. He led the attack at Pearl Harbour.

12. Six

13. Teeth

14. A mammal

15. The Antarctic

16. Jacob Roggeveen arrived there on Easter Sunday 1772.

17. Tend and keep it.

18. Sugar, Coconuts, Cotton, Gold and Cloth.

19. Fisi

20. The U.S.A. and part of it also belongs to Great Britain.

21. Volcanoes

22. Flying Foxes

23. The Rev John Williams

24. At least two hundred.

25. The First Born and The Pearl of the Pacific

26. Jesus Christ

27. Christian Fletcher